hello Toronto

GLC ✦ SILVER BURDETT
PUBLISHERS

ELMA SCHEMENAUER

Canada Rainbow Series
Cities

© 1986 **GLC Publishers Limited**
   115 Nugget Avenue
   Agincourt, Ontario M1S 3B1

All rights reserved. No part of this book may be copied or reproduced in any form or by any means without the written consent of the publisher.

Canadian Cataloguing in Publication Data
Schemenauer, Elma.
   Hello Toronto

(Canada rainbow series)
For use in schools.
Includes index.
ISBN 0-88874-261-4 (bound). — ISBN 0-88874-245-2 (pbk.). —
ISBN 0-88874-269-X (set, bound). — ISBN 0-88874-267-3
(set, pbk.)

1. Toronto (Ont.) — Juvenile literature.
I. Title. II. Series.

FC3097.33.S33 1986   j971.3'541   C85-099814-X
F1059.5.T684S33 1986

The Author
Elma Schemenauer is originally from Saskatchewan, and is presently living in Ontario. She has taught school in Saskatchewan and Nova Scotia, and has written a number of educational books for children.

Project Editor & Photo Research: *Deborah Lonergan*
Permissions Editor: *Estelle McGurk*
Design & Art Direction: *Holly Fisher & Associates*
Manuscript Reviewer: *Lois M. Harper*
Printed & Bound in Canada by: *Friesen Printers Ltd., Altona, Manitoba*

CREDITS
Cover Photo: W. Weaver/Hot Shots; City of Toronto Archives - P. Goodwin, photographer, pg. 6; Department of Regional Industrial Expansion photo, pgs. 9, 12, 13, 18, 20, 21, 22, 23, 26, 27, 28, 29; Deborah Drew-Brook-Cormack and Allan Cormack, pgs. 14, 15; J. G. Graphics, pg. 7; W. R. McCullagh/Miller Services, pg. 11; Metropolitan Toronto Library; T15196, pg. 16; Metropolitan Toronto Library: 976-21-1, pg. 17; Michele Nidenoff, pgs. 8, 10; SSC Photocentre — photo by George Hunter, pg. 25; Toronto Transit Commission, pg. 24.

hello

Toronto

Contents

How old is Toronto and how many people live there? 6

Where is Toronto and what does its name mean? 7

What is Toronto's tallest building? 8

What does Toronto Harbour look like? 9

What are some other important Toronto landmarks? 10

Why is Toronto's Yonge Street such an amazing street? 11

What rivers and wildlife are found in Toronto? 12

What kind of weather does Toronto have? 13

Who were the first Europeans in the Toronto area? 14

Who laid out streets and brought in the first settlers? 15

What was Toronto like in the days of the early settlers? 16

How did the city grow? 17

Why did government leaders form the Metro Toronto Council? 18

What kind of government does Metro Toronto have today? 19

What is Toronto like as a place to live and work? 20

What have immigrants from many lands brought to Toronto? 21

What happens at Caravan, Toronto's festival of cultures?   22

What are some other ways Torontonians have fun?   23

How do Torontonians get around their city?   24

What kinds of jobs in industry do people have in Toronto?   25

What other kinds of jobs do people have in Toronto?   26

What are some problems facing Toronto today?   27

How do Torontonians deal with their problems as a city?   28

What do Torontonians hope to do in the future?   29

Glossary   30

Index   32

Meet Seskwee Squirrel! In 1984 this lively little animal kicked off a big party. It was Toronto's birthday. The city was 150 years old. Like Seskwee Squirrel, the city of Toronto is lively. It is busy. And like the nut-gathering squirrel, it plans for the future.

Metropolitan Toronto is one of North America's fastest growing cities. About 3 000 000 people live there. This makes it the biggest city in Canada. Toronto is also the capital of the province of Ontario.

Seskwee Squirrel helped Toronto celebrate its Sesquicentennial (150th birthday) in 1984.

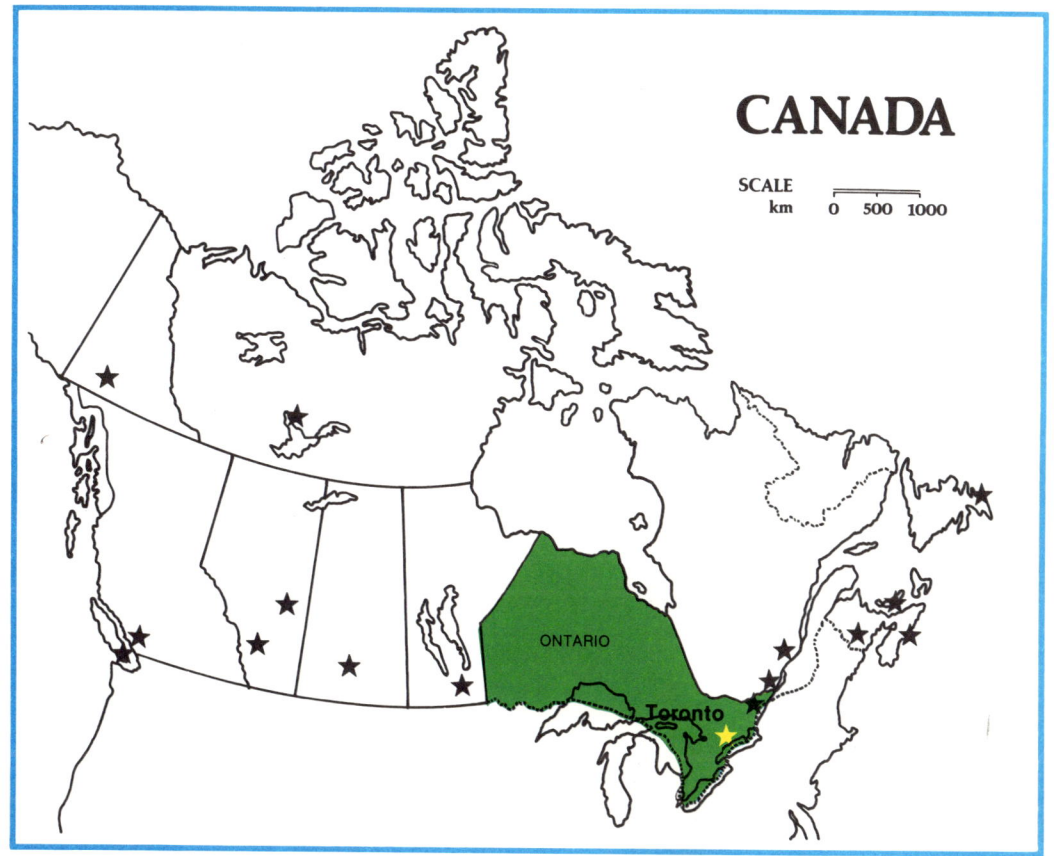

Meeting place — that's what the name *Toronto* means. It came from a Huron Indian word, long ago. Today, people meet in Toronto to trade, do business, produce goods, make films and movies, pass laws, study, write books, play sports, have fun, and more.

Toronto is in a key spot to be a meeting place. It is built on Lake Ontario's north shore. It is a main port on the long water highway known as the Great Lakes-St. Lawrence Seaway. In the countryside near Toronto is some of the richest farmland in Ontario. To Toronto's northeast and southwest, smaller cities and towns string out along the lakeshore.

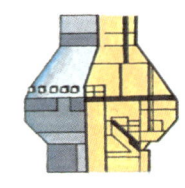

1 Space Deck
This is the world's highest look-out deck.

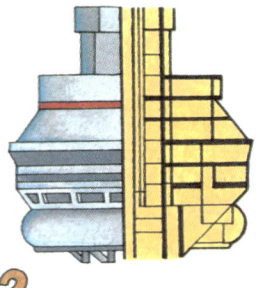

2 Sky Pod
A restaurant, look-out decks, and machinery are in the Sky Pod.

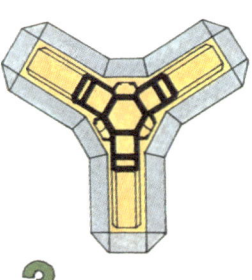

3 Foundation
Looking down the centre of the tower, you can see a stairway and four elevators.

4 Base
Stores and restaurants are at the base. A service area is underneath.

Downtown Toronto is built on a flat area of land by the lakeshore. Looking at the city's **skyline**, it is easy to forget the land is flat. There are so many high buildings! The CN Tower is the highest. Completed in 1975, it is the world's tallest **free-standing structure**. It holds **broadcasting antennas** for Toronto TV and FM radio stations. You can whiz up to the CN Tower's Sky Pod by high speed elevator.

Gazing down from the CN Tower's Sky Pod, you can see Toronto Harbour to the south. It is a broad stretch of calm water. Ships from all over the world dock there.

Sheltering the harbour is a group of islands shaped like a fish hook. These are the Toronto Islands. They are a good place to take a picnic on a hot summer day!

Toronto from the air.

What could you see and do on a walk up Yonge Street? Which downtown Toronto area would you choose to explore first?

From high in the CN Tower, you can see other Toronto **landmarks**. There are the bank towers, headquarters of Canadian banks. There is the glassy Eaton Centre, a shopping mall that looks like a giant greenhouse. There is Toronto's **ultramodern** City Hall with its two curving towers and **reflecting pool**. North of City Hall are three major hospitals — Toronto General, Mount Sinai, and the Hospital for Sick Children. North of the hospitals are the green-roofed Ontario Parliament Buildings. Near by is the University of Toronto, Canada's largest university. York University is near the north edge of the city.

The busy corner of Yonge and Bloor Streets in Toronto. Where does Yonge Street start? Where does it end?

What is the world's longest street? The *Guinness Book of World Records* says it's Toronto's Yonge Street. This amazing street starts at the lakeshore. Then it just keeps on going, north out of the city almost 2000 km to Rainy River, Ontario. Another name for it is Highway 11.

Yonge Street forms Toronto's "spine." It divides Toronto into an eastern and a western half. The streets are laid out mostly in a **rectangular grid** pattern. This makes it easy for people to find their way around.

A polar bear goes for a swim at the Metro Toronto Zoo.

Many fluffy tailed squirrels like Seskwee scamper through Toronto's parks and back yards. The city also has lots of other wildlife — raccoons, rabbits, chipmunks, gulls, cardinals, blue jays. For such a large city, Toronto is surprisingly rich in birds and small animals. One reason is that it has three rivers. These rivers and their branches run through wooded valleys and ravines, which make good homes for wildlife.

    The Humber River flows through the western edge of Toronto. The Don River angles through the centre. The steep-banked Rouge River cuts through the eastern part of the city. In the valley of the Rouge is the large and beautiful Metro Toronto Zoo.

Toronto's weather makes it a fairly comfortable city to live in. Usually there is enough rain, but not too much. Winters are not as cold as in many other Canadian cities. Partly this is because it is quite far south. Most people are surprised to learn that Toronto is at about the same **latitude** as Rome, Italy. Average temperature for January is about -5°C. Summers in Toronto are pleasant except during the city's sticky heat waves. Average temperature for July is about 22°C.

Enjoying the summer weather outside Toronto's famous castle, Casa Loma. These people belong to a club that acts out scenes from the days of knights and castles.

Etienne Brûlé, known as the first coureur de bois. Brûlé was the first European to see the area we now call Toronto.

Etienne Brûlé was a young French adventurer dressed in buckskin. He was the first European to see the area we now call Toronto. The year was 1615.

At the time, the Toronto area was a great marsh, overgrown with a tangle of trees. The French did not care much for this swampy area of laughing loons. They were more interested in the Humber River as a trade route. It wasn't until 1720 that French traders finally set up a trading post at the river's mouth.

By the late 1700s the English had taken over. They bought the Toronto area from the Mississauga Indians, paying for it with blankets, hatchets, cloth, and beads. In 1793 it became the capital of Upper Canada (later Ontario). Lieutenant-Governor John Graves Simcoe set up his headquarters there. He brought in settlers. He laid out streets, including Yonge Street.

Simcoe called his capital York. Settlers, struggling with the mud and mosquitoes, called it Muddy York.

It wasn't always easy — being a settler in Simcoe's Muddy York.

Engine Number 2 of the Ontario, Simcoe, and Huron Rail Road about 1880. How did railways affect Toronto?

How muddy was York? Early settlers used to tell this joke: "If you see a hat on the street, you'd better look under it. You'll probably find a horse and rider sunken into the mud!"

In spite of the mud, Simcoe's settlement grew. By 1834 it had over 9000 people. In that year it became a city and took back its old name: Toronto. A fiery, newspaper-publishing Scot, William Lyon Mackenzie, became the city's first mayor.

In the 1850s, railways were built through Toronto. The city became the centre of a great **network** of railway lines. True to its name, Toronto was becoming a meeting place for people from near and far.

During the early years, many little settlements sprang up along Toronto's north-south "spine," Yonge Street. Yorkville, Deer Park, Davisville, Eglinton, and Bedford Park were some of these. As the city grew, it swallowed up these little towns and villages. Outside the city itself, still more townships grew up. By 1950 there were 12 of these surrounding townships.

G.E. Coon general store at the northwest corner of Yonge Street and Eglinton Avenue in the 1920s.

In the early 1950s, both Toronto and its surrounding townships began having a lot of problems. They had all grown so fast. **Local** governments had found it hard to keep up with their people's needs. Some people had no sidewalks or **sewers**. Some needed schools, hospitals, highways, parks, or shopping centres. Toronto and the townships around it decided they could face the **challenges** better if they joined together. In 1953 they did this, forming the Metro Toronto Council.

On the left, Toronto City Hall. In winter, the pool in front of it becomes a skating rink.

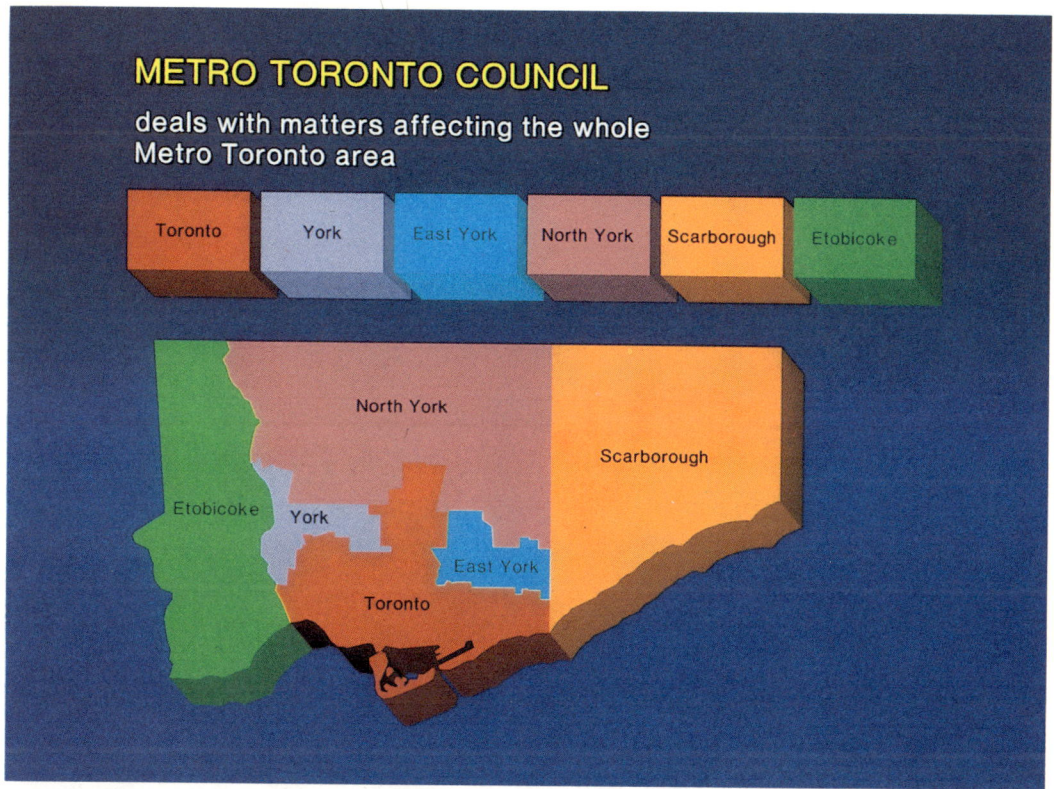

The Metro Toronto type of government was the first of its kind to be set up in North America. It has two levels. The Metro Toronto Council looks after matters affecting the whole Metro Toronto area; for example, traffic planning. The separate areas of Metro also have their own governments. These deal with matters affecting them only; for example, laws about how houses must be built.

In 1967 Metro Toronto **reorganized** itself. Instead of Toronto and 12 *townships*, it became Toronto and five *boroughs*: York, East York, North York, Scarborough, and Etobicoke. In the 1980s most of these boroughs have become *cities*.

Boy meets raccoon at the Royal Ontario Museum. Torontonians are proud of this famous museum, often called the ROM.

"The Toronto **subway** is so *clean!*" Visitors often say this when riding the city's fast underground trains. Toronto's people are proud of their clean city. They are proud of their many trees and gardens. They are also proud that their city is such a safe, orderly place to live and work.

Some people think Toronto cares a bit too much about order, laws, rules, and doing things the "proper" way. They think Torontonians should loosen up a little. They should not take themselves so seriously. They should be friendlier, more exciting, more daring!

For years people have seen Toronto as a city that did not know how to have fun. But that's changing quickly. **Immigration** has helped. Since World War II, people from many lands have poured into Toronto and made their homes there. They've come from Italy, Israel, Germany, Portugal, Hungary, Korea, India, Greece, South America, China, the West Indies, and many other places. **Immigrants** bring their songs, dances, colourful costumes, and good cooking. They bring new ideas about how to live and have fun.

A costume at Caribana. This lively festival celebrates the culture of immigrants from the West Indies.

Torontonians enjoy each other's many different **cultures**. Every year in June, Toronto holds a festival of cultures. It is called Caravan. Visitors buy "passports" that allow them to go on "world tours." Moving from building to building, they can join in Polish folk dancing, listen to Caribbean steel band music, learn the Japanese art of paper folding (called origami), or visit a Ukrainian Orthodox Church. They can eat Italian lasagna, Scottish shortbread, Native Canadian bannock and moose stew, and much more.

Dancers at Caravan. The festival's different buildings and tents, called "pavilions," are scattered throughout the city.

"OK, Blue Jays. Let's play ball!" Torontonians also have fun in other ways. They love to watch their baseball team, the Blue Jays. They enjoy watching Maple Leafs hockey games, and Argonauts football games.

Down on the lakeshore, Torontonians enjoy visiting Harbourfront, Ontario Place, and the yearly Canadian National Exhibition, or "Ex." They enjoy music in the city's many concert halls, such as Roy Thomson Hall. They enjoy plays in the city's many theatres, such as the Royal Alexandra.

In the Ontario Science Centre, they talk to computers, see **laser beams** cut through bricks, and stand their hair on end with 500 000 **volts** of electricity!

Log-sawing at the Canadian National Exhibition. Besides the "Ex," what other places can people go for fun in Toronto?

"Take the TTC, the better way." Many Torontonians use the Toronto Transit Commission system to get around their city. The system includes buses, streetcars, and speedy subway trains. The new SRT (Scarborough Rapid Transit) line links the city of Scarborough with the subway and downtown Toronto. GO (Government of Ontario) trains run beyond the borders of Metropolitan Toronto. They link Toronto with nearby cities, such as Richmond Hill and Hamilton.

A lot of Torontonians also own and drive cars. A computer controls the traffic lights on the city's many streets. Traffic planning and repairing the city's huge **expressways** are constant challenges for the Metro Toronto Council.

A streetcar in downtown Toronto's Chinatown. The sign shows you can take this streetcar to Parliament Street.

"The jobs brought the people, and the people brought the jobs." People who came to Toronto after World War II were looking for jobs. They found them. But the new immigrants also needed goods and services. As so often happens, their needs created more jobs.

Industry is the making of goods. It provides many jobs for Torontonians. Among the things they make are: computers, TV sets, radios, stoves, toys, games, scientific instruments, furniture, and clothes. Many Torontonians also work in food industries. For example, they pack meat and produce baked goods.

Yummy! Making candy at Rowntree Mackintosh Ltd. in Toronto. What other things do Torontonians make?

Toronto is the communications centre of Canada. This means it has many jobs for people who work in broadcasting, printing, and publishing. The city is also the money and business centre of Canada. This means it has jobs for bankers, stock brokers, accountants, secretaries, and store clerks.

More and more, Toronto is becoming a tourist centre. "Clean but exciting" and "safe but fun" — this is how people describe it. As a tourist centre, Toronto provides jobs for tour guides, restaurant **employees**, and **transportation** workers.

The Toronto Stock Exchange. Why does Toronto have many jobs for people such as stock brokers and bankers?

Traffic roars along the many-laned 401 highway. The 401 runs east-west through the northern part of Metro Toronto.

"The City That Works" is what many people call Toronto. However, like any fast growing city, it has some growing pains. These are some of the questions local government leaders ask themselves: What shall we do about pollution from our many cars and factories? How many more super highways shall we build? How can we provide enough housing for all our people? Which old buildings shall we tear down? Which ones shall we fix up and keep? What shall we do with Yonge Street, the Toronto Islands, and the waterfront?

Inside the Eaton Centre. Built in the 1970s, it has shops, theatres, and restaurants on many different levels.

Torontonians do not always agree on the answers. However, they keep working towards solutions. They have solved past problems in some interesting ways.

For instance, in the 1970s, builders were constructing the Eaton Centre. The Church of the Holy Trinity was in the way. Plans called for it to be bulldozed down. However, a small group of people fought to save the church, one of Toronto's oldest houses of worship. They won. Building plans were even changed to make sure the church would continue to get enough sunshine!

Toronto is a city of many names. It has been called York, Muddy York, Toronto the Good, City of Churches, Hogtown, the Changing City, People City, the City That Works.

All these names fit in their own way. And in a way the glassy Eaton Centre and the old stone Church of the Holy Trinity stand as important **symbols** of Toronto. The city is a special blend of the new and the old. Torontonians hope they can keep the right blend as they move into the future.

The old, triangular "Flatiron Building" with the ultramodern CN Tower in the background.

Glossary

broadcasting antenna — A wire, rod, or other metal device used to send TV or radio signals (p. 8).

challenge — A call to take part in a contest or struggle (p. 18).

culture — The way of living and/or the artistic products of a group of people. Also fineness of manners, taste, feelings, and so on (p. 22).

employee — A person paid to work for some person or company (p. 26).

expressway — A big main highway for fast travel, often having several lanes (p. 24).

free-standing — Standing by itself; having no wires attached to steady it (p. 8).

immigrant — A person who comes from one country to settle in another (p. 21).

immigration — The process of coming from one country to settle in another (p. 21).

landmark — A famous building, statue, mountain, or other important, easily seen feature of an area (p. 10).

laser beam — A kind of strong narrow ray of light. A laser beam can be used to bore holes in hard substances such as metal (p. 23).

latitude — The distance north or south of the equator. It is measured in degrees. For example, Toronto's latitude is about 43 degrees north. Rome's latitude is nearly 42 degrees north (p. 13).

local — Having to do with a certain place or places (p. 18).

Metropolitan Toronto — The area including the main city of Toronto, as well as Scarborough (to the east), Etobicoke (to the west), and York, East York, and North York (to the north). A government body called the Metro Toronto Council deals with matters affecting this whole area (p. 6).

network — Any netlike system of things; for example, a network of cracks in a sidewalk (p. 16).

rectangular grid — A system of lines forming shapes having four sides and four right angles (p. 11).

reflecting pool — A small body of still water that acts something like a mirror, showing images of what is above and around it (p. 10).

reorganized — Organized again; arranged in a new way (p. 19).

sewer — A drain pipe used to carry away waste material, usually underground (p. 18).

skyline — The outline of buildings, trees, and so on, as seen against the sky (p. 8).

structure — Something that has been built, such as a house (p. 8).

subway — An electric railway running completely or mostly underground beneath city streets (p. 20).

symbol — An object, sign, or picture that stands for something else. For example, the lion is a symbol of courage (p. 29).

transportation — The method or methods of carrying people and things from one place to another (p. 26).

ultramodern — Very up-to-date (p. 10).

volt — A unit used to measure electrical power (p. 23).

Index

arts and entertainment
 7, 8, 23
Brûlé, Etienne 14
Caravan 22
churches and religion 28, 29
climate 13
CN Tower 8–10
downtown 8, 10, 11, 24
education and schools 10, 18
entertainment and arts
 7, 8, 23
future 6, 29
government (city) 18, 19, 24
government (provincial) 6, 10
harbour 7, 9, 27
history 14–18
hospitals 10, 18
houses 19, 27
jobs (work) 7, 25, 26
Lake Ontario 7, 8
location 7, 8
Mackenzie, William Lyon 16
Muddy York 15, 16
names for Toronto
 7, 15, 27, 29
Native people 7, 15, 22
Ontario Science Centre 23
people 6, 7, 15, 20–25
population 6, 16
problems 18, 27, 28
religion and churches 28, 29
rivers 12, 14
schools and education 10, 18
Seskwee Squirrel 6, 12

settlers 15–17
ships 9
Simcoe, John Graves 15, 16
sports 7, 23
squirrels 6, 12
Toronto Islands 9, 27
traders 14, 15
transportation 7, 16, 20,
 24, 27
weather 13
work (jobs) 7, 25, 26
Yonge Street 11, 15, 17, 27
York 15, 16

Bibliothèque Municipale
STURGEON FALLS
Public Library